AF574090

INDIAN SUMMER OF STEAM

46143

INDIAN SUMMER OF STEAM

D.R.Hagan

LONDON

IAN ALLAN LTD

Cover: 'Jubilee' class 4-6-0s at Penrith station on 22 July 1961. No 45681 *Aboukir* pulls out with the 'Saints and Sinners Special' from Keswick to Euston, whilst No 45655 *Keith* waits to take the 9.18am (SO) from Keswick on to Manchester and Crewe.

Dedicated to the memory of
Bishop Eric Treacy

First published 1980

ISBN 0 7110 1025 0

Published by Ian Allan Ltd, Shepperton, Surrey; and printed by Ian Allan Printing Ltd at their works at Coombelands in Runnymede, England

Introduction

Efforts to analyse the fascination of steam, and for that matter railways in general, are difficult. It is obvious that steam meant different things to different people. The majestic qualities of steam power cast a spell upon many which other forms of traction have not been able to achieve. Steam locomotives personified power in a special manner. Like the carthorse the steam engine visually struggled 'to get to grips' with its load. The release of steam from the safety valves bore witness to the pent up energy stored in the boiler. One could sense, and sometimes feel, the thrust of the pistons under the graceful direction of the rods controlling the passage of steam. Steam locomotives also possessed a personality and individuality that defied engineering logic. In fact, it could be claimed that of all the machines created by man they come closest to being a living thing. Furthermore their day to day performance could be attributed to the skill and determination of the men who drove them, many of whom developed an uncanny feel for the mood of the machine.

My own first real interest in steam was aroused in about 1951 by the magnificent spectacle of spotless 'Britannias' 'flying' through Marden with the up 'Golden Arrow'. Two years later a school trip to Euston and Paddington opened up a new world. Luckily my parents then went to live in central London and I was able to visit various terminal stations, which in a way became the citadels of all that I had begun to worship. The sight of 'Jubilees' gliding into St Pancras framed by the magnificent canopy roof, the volcanic eruption of 'Kings' pulling out of Paddington, and the gloom of Kings Cross, brightened only by the shafts of sunlight filtering through the smoke, are visual experiences which will live with me for the rest of my life.

Aspirations to retain this atmosphere led me naturally to photography. However, it was a chance purchase of Bishop Eric Treacy's book *Steam Up*, which fired my enthusiasm and provided my working standard. It was to take five years' toil and tribulation with inadequate equipment and grainy negatives, before my ambitions were realised. The turning point came in 1957 when I went to Doncaster Locomotive Works as a trade apprentice. In those days apprentices were paid about £3 a week, to work from seven thirty until five thirty, with 50p extra for Saturday morning. My parents paid for my digs and from my wages I managed to save up and buy an Agfa Isolette, using a 120 film size, and having a maximum shutter speed of 1/500sec. To a young apprentice on limited funds, without a car at his disposal, the choice was for busy locations within easy reach by rail. To a certain degree luck was on my side; my family settled in Kent, I served my apprenticeship at Doncaster, went to college at Derby and holidayed at the homes of two aunts in Devon. My perfectionistic approach led me to miss many golden opportunities, but led me to my goal. For instance I rarely took photographs when the sun wasn't shining, put my camera away during the winter, gave no thought to unusual angles; and avoided 35mm cameras and their lens flexibility. I continued to use $2\frac{1}{4}$in square format as a means of limiting grain on the prints. This process being further enhanced by the use of a relatively slow film, namely FP3 (now FP4), which was developed in 'Promicrol' developer. Naturally enough a slow film with a fast shutter speed necessitated opening up the aperture to f8-f5.6. The use of the latter stop led to aberration of the lens which can be identified by a sharp fall-off in focus on the outer regions of the negatives. I countered this problem by buying myself a Roliecord VA camera in 1960, which also had a relatively slow shutter speed of 1/500sec. However, this limitation was no real problem as trains at speed did not produce the type of smoke effects that I was seeking. The other constraint of great importance was the imposed depth of field ie the field of sharp focus. The use of low apertures cuts the field down and for this reason I had to choose vantage points which kept the foreground at a safe distance. I did not use filters to enhance the sky and cloud effects as it obviously compounds the aperture and depth of field problems; and in my experience the sky can be doctored during the printing phase by vignetting.

Those sparkling prints of the 'Bishop' had become my obsession and I pursued this goal relentlessly. However, it soon became clear that a lineside pass was essential, even if the smoke abatement laws had all but ended arranged smoke screens. As I was within easy reach of Doncaster, Sheffield, Leeds and York, these junctions soon proved to be ideal hunting grounds. With this new found freedom the location developed a new dimension, but it was finally the lure of Shap which proved to be irresistible and provided the source of sparkling prints. I've heard it said that it always rained at Shap. In many ways this is true; but when the sun shone it was a railway photographer's dream.

By 1965, saddened by the demise of steam, I put my camera away and concentrated on other pursuits. In this way I missed the final phase of steam operation, and as a result this pictorial record has been titled 'Indian Summer of Steam'. So let's drift back into the days when steam reigned supreme.

I would like to express my appreciation to Allan Bray and Paul Davis for proof reading the captions and for their suggestions on the material contained in them.

Duncan Hagan

Uxbridge
Middlesex

May 1979

Classic Lines

Top left: 'Castle' class 4-6-0 No 7019 *Fowey Castle* shatters the serenity of Sonning Cutting as it hurtles through with a Weston-super-Mare-Paddington express on 22 July 1959.

Left: 'King Arthur' No 30806 *Sir Galleron* threading its way through the Garden of England on the outskirts of Faversham. The train is the 9.35am Victoria-Ramsgate and the date 28 March 1959.

Top: One of the Eastern's royal engines awaits her next turn of duty at Liverpool Street on 2 August 1958. The engine is a Thompson conversion of Gresley's B17 class. Re-classified B2, No 61671 was named *Royal Sovereign.*

Above: A SECR Class D patiently awaiting retirement and preservation at Stewarts Lane mpd on 25 June 1958. No 31737 was withdrawn in 1956 and restored to its former glory at Ashford during 1960, and is now on display at York Railway Museum.

Top: A mighty BR 9F No 92133 trundles through Elstree with an up loose coupled goods train on 11 March 1961. In many ways this class represented the climax of British steam engine development. Equally at home on freight or express passenger turns; coupled with ease of maintenance and freedom from design faults, it represented the ultimate compromise.

Above: The beautiful lines of No 6021 *King Richard II* grace the head end of the 11.10am Paddington-Birmingham on 9 August 1962. The train is approaching Old Oak Common and is about to branch off the West of England main line.

Right: The 'Jubilee' class 4-6-0 had a mixed reputation under BR ownership, but there was no denying their pleasing lines. No 45597 *Barbados* at rest by the Derby shed turntable on 7 October 1962.

BARBADOS

General Purpose 4-6-0s

Left: 'Royal Scot' class 4-6-0 No 46143 *The South Staffordshire Regiment* thunders out of Kensal Green Tunnel with a Euston-Liverpool express on 24 July 1959. Claimed by many to be one of the finest British 4-6-0s the 'Royal Scots' had powerful looks to support this claim.

Below: The classic 4-6-0s were undoubtedly the 'Castles' and 'Kings', and in this picture No 7027 *Thornbury Castle* threads her way out of Oxford station on 5 September 1962, with a Hereford-Paddington train.

Right: It could be said of the B1s that they possessed functional simplicity without the austere lines that dominated at the time of their construction. Intended as a standard design for the LNER they worked far afield on all types of duties. Here No 61074 coasts into Sheffield Victoria with the 2.20pm from Nottingham on 26 June 1960.

Below right: No 6849 *Walton Grange* in charge of what was claimed by the signalman to be a workingman's train from Plymouth to the west on 9 September 1959. The 'Grange' was a direct descendant of Churchward's 'Saint' class having smaller wheels, and can be classified as a general purpose 4-6-0 of noble origin.

61074
6849

Top: The B16 was one of the best 4-6-0 designs turned out by the North Eastern Railway, who were the first railway to use 4-6-0s for passenger work. Despite their heavy coal consumption and their knack of cracking frames, they survived up until the final years of steam operation. In this picture No 61418 strides away from York with an unidentified up train on 25 June 1960.

Above: Some of Maunsell's 'King Arthurs' of 1925 were nicknamed 'Scotsmen', by virtue of the fact that they were manufactured by the North British Loco Co of Glasgow. His blastpipe/chimney improvements cured the erratic steaming problems of Urie's design, thus creating a very capable engine. In this picture No 30457 *Sir Bedivere* heads the 9.45am Waterloo-Southampton train (24 July 1959).

Four-Coupled Maid-of-all-Work

Top: Renowned for their speed the T9 class earned themselves the nickname of 'Greyhounds'. Despite her age No 30715 appears to be in fine fettle whilst in charge of the Plymouth portion of the up 'Atlantic Coast Express'. Photographed near Tamerton Foliot on 9 September 1959.

Above: Another very successful 4-4-0, noted for its turn of speed, was the GCR 'Director' class which was perpetuated by the LNER for use in Scotland. In this picture a 'Large Director', of 1920 GCR origin, plods out of Doncaster with the Sundays only 5.43pm Cleethorpes-Sheffield train on 20 July 1958. No 62666 was named *Zeebrugge* and survived until February 1961.

Left: No 62727 *The Quorn* awaiting clearance from Wortley Junction box before backing down on to a waiting train at Leeds Central station on 4 July 1959. The 'Hunts' were one of Gresley's less successful designs and were notorious for their high maintenance costs.

Below: The 'Midland Compounds' were noted for their speed and economy, and were the last British engines to work on the compound principle, other than experimental versions. In this picture No 41068, one of Holbeck's compounds, takes charge of a St Pancras-Bradford train for the last leg of the journey between Leeds and Bradford on 16 August 1958.

Left: Maunsell's 'Schools' were the most powerful 4-4-0 in the world. They were really a scaled down three cylinder 'Nelson/ Arthur' designed to meet the motive power requirements of the Hastings line. These very successful engines entered service in 1930 and survived until 1961/62. In this picture No 30930 *Radley* coasts through Ashford with the 2.20pm Deal-Charing Cross on 16 July 1960.

Pacifics of the Big Four

Above: Thompson succeeded Gresley as CM&EE of the LNER and set out to discredit his former boss. One such act was to cancel the last four V2s and use the parts to build A2 Pacifics. The result was not a great success, they were capable of accelerating faster than the A4s, but had a higher specific fuel consumption and a tendency to crack frames. No 60513 *Dante* fulfils a rather humdrum duty with the 7am Peterborough-Kings Cross semi-fast on 10 June 1961, photographed approaching Holloway South up box.

Below: During the early 1950s the A3s had sunk in status and were regarded as second class power. However, the fitment of double chimneys and Kylchap double blastpipes, between 1958 and 1960, put them back on the heaviest express turns. No 60062 *Minoru* restarts from Doncaster with the York portion of the 4.05pm from Kings Cross on 28 June 1960.

Above: A 'West Country' class Pacific No 34092 *City of Wells* on the down 'Golden Arrow' approaching Ashford on 19 July 1960. Bulleid's lightweight Pacifics were affectionately known as 'spam cans', by virtue of the airsmoothed casing, which was the shape of a tin of 'Cornell' spam. This feature was primarily intended to allow the engine to be driven through a carriage washing plant.

Centre right: No 46232 *Duchess of Montrose* was built as a non-streamlined engine. Those that had the streamlined casing incurred a 2 ton weight penalty, and a feature which was of little practical benefit in daily service. On Saturday 22 July 1961, the engine was at the head of the 9.15am Crewe-Glasgow train, and is shown crossing Eamont viaduct on the northern side of Shap.

Bottom right: The 'Princess' Pacifics were built to run non-stop between London and Glasgow with 500 ton trains. Twenty-eight years later we find No 46200 *The Princess Royal* still fulfilling this role whilst pulling the 10.15am Glasgow-Euston express up the northern slopes of Shap on 24 June 1961. Not for long however, as this engine was withdrawn just over a year later.

Engines that Won the War

Above: A three-cylinder staccato beat echoes around York racecourse as V2 No 60983 pounds out of York with the 'Scarborough Flyer' on 25 June 1960. During the war these engines regularly worked 25-coach trains weighing approximately 850 tons. In this instance she is coping with a mere 14 coaches.

Centre left: The 'Black Fives' were also known as the engines that won the war. In this instance No 44713 wheezes up Shap with a parcels train. These engines were brilliant all-rounders and were very popular with all who came in contact with them.

Bottom left: Some of Robinson's 2-8-0s of 1911 were adopted in 1917 by the Railway Operating Division (ROD) for military use, and ended up serving overseas in both world wars. Perhaps the greatest tribute to them was the fact that the GWR purchased some after World War I where they survived for 35 years. Pictured here is No 63664 approaching Lincoln on 20 September 1958.

Austerity Fashion

Top: Another very successful engine born of wartime demand was the Ministry of Supply 'Austerity' design of 1943, examples of which ended up all over the world. Rarely seen on passenger stock, No 90009 puts in an appearance at Doncaster on 5 July 1960 with an empty stock working.

Above: Bulleid's Q1 0-6-0 design was also conceived during the war and was basic as well as ugly. Nevertheless it was a very successful engine. In this picture No 33036 comes off the Maidstone line at Ashford with what the headcode described as a Bricklayers' Arms-Maidstone East-Dover goods train.

Left: To some degree the Ivatt 2-6-0 and its sister 2-6-2T must have been based upon the earlier indifferent Fowler and Stanier 2-6-2T designs. However, the third attempt proved to be a very sound one, once the draughting problem had been solved on the Swindon stationary plant. No 41245 shunting empty stock at Sheffield Midland on 5 December 1959.

Below: After the war the LMS operating authorities would have continued to order Fowler's 4F 0-6-0 freight engines. However, Ivatt managed to obtain authority to build a 2-6-0 design incorporating many modern features aimed at easy maintenance namely, a self cleaning smokebox, a rocking grate, self emptying hopper ashpans, etc. Again draughting proved a problem, but once solved the engines proved their worth. No 43110 was photographed at Lincoln with an empty stock working on 22 August 1959.

The Standards

Above: The BR Class 2 2-6-2T was a direct descendant of Ivatt's 2-6-2T of 1946. The engine in question has been fitted with push and pull equipment as were others of this class. No 84020 is propelling the 3.19pm Maidstone East-Ashford local and is approaching Ashford on 20 July 1959.

Right: Another Ashford-Maidstone East local, the 3.11pm in this instance, in the capable hands of a BR Class 4 2-6-4T No 80064 on 16 July 1960. These engines were designed and built at Brighton and were a development of Fairburn's 2-6-4T design of 1945 with smaller cylinders and increased boiler pressure. They too were noted for acceleration, speed and fuel economy.

Top: The BR Class 3 2-6-2T and its tender twin 2-6-0 of the 77000 series were introduced to cope with traffic beyond the capability of the Class 2 variants on lines where a 16 ton axle load limit existed. However, improvements to the routes concerned made this class unnecessary. No 82011 takes water at Tipton St Johns on 10 September 1958 before continuing with the 5.20pm Sidmouth Junction-Sidmouth local.

Above: A very popular standard was the versatile 'go anywhere' Class 4 4-6-0 tender engine. This was a development of Fairburn's 2-6-4T with a tender to increase its operating range. On this occasion No 75023 is assisted up the Lickey Incline by a GWR pannier tank No 9493 with the 7.47am Gloucester Eastgate-Birmingham train on 25 July 1961.

Left: The climax of the Churchward/Stanier development of taper boilers was reached when the Doncaster designed Class 5 4-6-0 was introduced in 1951. Like the 'Black Fives' they proved to be reliable and capable machines. No 73082 accelerates the 3.22pm Ramsgate-Victoria train away from Faversham on 26 March 1959.

Below: The other BR Class 4 2-6-0 tender engine was virtually a copy of Ivatt's 2-6-0 design of 1947, but incorporating standard fittings and a more aesthetic appearance. No 76012 gathers speed with an up special by Allbrook box, Eastleigh, on 6 August 1960.

Top: A BR Class 9F 2-10-0 No 92143 eases into Doncaster past Carr Depot on 1 September 1961 with a return working of an Aberdeen-Kings Cross fish van train. In all 251 of these fine engines were built at Swindon and Crewe between 1953 and 1960.

Above: An immaculate Cardiff Canton BR Class 7 Pacific No 70023 *Venus* on the up 'Red Dragon' in Sonning Cutting on 22 July 1959. When first introduced to the Western Region these engines were heartily disliked by the conservative Western crews, but they eventually found favour at Cardiff Canton where they acquitted themselves well on the Cardiff-Paddington expresses.

Old Stagers Live On

Top: A veteran of 1907, namely a Class C14 4-4-2T, shunts its coaches into a bay platform at Doncaster before departing with a local for Penistone on 18 June 1959; 10 days before the withdrawal of this service. No 67445 was a Robinson Great Central design and was built for the suburban service out of Marylebone. The engine was one of the last survivors of the class being withdrawn in March of 1960.

Above: A GNR Class C12 4-4-2T No 67365, dating back to 1898, awaiting the cutter's torch at Doncaster Plant Works on 4 June 1958. Built for the GNR suburban service out of Kings Cross where they were no match for their rivals the Stirling 0-4-4T of the 1880s, but survived to work the Essendine-Stamford branch until 1958.

Top: Beattie's well tank of 1874 was really an antiquity ideally suited to a special role. Three of these engines worked the China Clay traffic on the lightly laid branches from Wadebridge to Wenford Bridge and Ruthern Bridge; to be finally displaced by GWR pannier tanks in December of 1962. No 30585 is shown at Eastleigh depot on 5 August 1960.

Above: This SECR Class R1 0-6-0T No 31337 was a Stirling design of 1888 and spent its latter years in the company of two other R class tanks struggling up a 1 in 30 gradient, from Folkestone harbour, hauling boat trains. The engine behind is a Class 01 0-6-0 No 31370 dating from 1878, but extensively rebuilt in 1903. Both engines were awaiting scrapping at Ashford Works on 18 April 1960.

32646
OP
32646

Top left: Many tank engines lingered on because they continued to fulfil an unchanging specialised role reliably. One such case was the A1X class, known as 'Terriers', who worked the Havant branch. Built in 1872 for the LBSCR, and rebuilt in 1911, the last one was not withdrawn until 1963, leaving no less than 10 out of the 50 preserved.

Left: A 'Compound' No 40907 of Millhouses depot assists a BR Class 5 No 73016 back to the depot. This famous design was perpetuated by the LMS as a result of prejudice rather than foresight for the future traffic requirements. However, they were tested against alternative 4-6-0 designs of the day, and were found to be fast, economical and versatile.

Top: The A5s were actually designed for freight work in 1911, but were unsuitable due to insufficient braking power. After the formation of the LNER a further batch were introduced in 1925 for suburban service out of Marylebone. No 69820 marshals its stock for the 3pm Lincoln-Nottingham-Derby train on 22 August 1959 at Lincoln St Marks.

Above: Some of these Midland 0-6-0s dating from 1885 survived until the end of steam working on the ex-Midland lines. Here No 43658 pauses by Way and Works box Derby after a break in her humdrum duties in which she hauled a LCGB tour on Sunday 7 October 1962.

Freight Traffic in Recession

Top: Riddles' 'Austerity' design was born of the needs of war. Ease of assembly and manufacture of component parts was an essential design feature. The engines could be built in half the time required for a Stanier 8F. 935 were built and all but three were shipped to Europe in 1944/45; with some 533 returning after the war. No 90180 is shown here leaving York with an up freight on 25 June 1960.

Above: Despite its inherent design weaknesses the MR Class 4F 0-6-0s continued to multiply between 1911 and 1941 until no less than 772 were in service. The fact remains that despite poor front end design and axlebox weaknesses they suited the traffic department needs admirably. In this instance No 44599 pounds past Little Eaton Junction with an up goods on 12 October 1960.

Top: A 'Manor' class 4-6-0 No 7816 *Frilsham Manor* comes off the Royal Albert Bridge, Saltash, with a down goods on 9 September 1959, essentially they were designed for secondary line duty, in particular the Cambrian section. Their design was based on the 'Grange' but with a lighter boiler and incorporating parts from withdrawn Class 4300 2-6-0s, which were too heavy to work this section.

Above: Class O2 2-8-0 No 63922 eases a down freight past Bridge Junction box, Doncaster, on 2 May 1959. Appearing in 1918, the O2 was the first locomotive to be fitted with conjugate valve gear. These three cylinder units were found to be more economical than their two-cylinder predecessors of 1913, and became the standard LNER heavy freight engine.

Above: The Great Western 2-8-0 was the first engine in the world to use the Consolidation wheel arrangement. The prototype appeared in 1903 and successive batches followed until 1942, thus establishing the soundness of the design. No 3864 on a down coal train running along the Exe Estuary at Starcross on 11 September 1958.

Below: A Class N 2-6-0 No 31863 ambles through Ashford station with an up goods train on 20 July 1959. These popular engines fulfilled a multitude of roles and were often seen on 15-coach troop trains during World War II, and in peacetime they sometimes appeared on the 'Kentish Belle' Pullman train.

Tank Engines Galore

Above: Class 5100 2-6-2T No 4117 at speed with the 11am Exeter-Dartmouth train between Exton and Starcross on 8 September 1958. The 'Prairie' tank was another GWR engine whose build dates spanned a long period, namely 46 years. Interesting features are the struts that support the buffer beam for such duties as banking and the sloping tops on the side tanks to improve vision.

Below: Another old-timer looking none the worse for wear after 70 years service is O2 class 0-4-4T No 30193 leaving Bere Alston on 7 September 1959 with the 12.50pm Bere Alston-Plymouth local.

HIGGS
LEEDS
42349
68528

Top left: Early LMS engines suffered as a result of the Midland dominance. However, their 2-6-4T was an exception and this fine design formed the basis for the Stanier and Fairburn 2-6-4Ts which followed. Part of their success stemmed from the Horwich influence on valve gear, front end and axlebox design. No 42349 is pulling empty stock away from Sheffield Midland on 15 August 1959.

Left: A 56-year old Class J69 potters about shunting at Lincoln on 20 September 1958. Looking at No 68528 it is difficult to realise that these diminutive tank engines were one of the mainstays of the GER's highly efficient suburban system. One can only imagine the sight of them at the head of 15 four wheelers, containing up to 750 passengers hurtling down the bank to Clapton Junction at 60mph, and all for two pence return to Chingford!

Above: A Class H 0-4-4T No 31544 setting off from Tonbridge with the 4.38pm to Oxted on 24 June 1958. These Wainwright engines were introduced for suburban traffic on the SECR. They worked all over the eastern section of the Southern Region and most survived until early 1960.

Steam on Shed

Top left: A 'Ragtimer' simmers away peacefully in the evening sun as it approaches the end of its life. These mixed traffic engines were very successful but were quickly overshadowed by the larger boiler version classified K3. Probably best known for the work that they performed on the steeply graded West Highland line. No 61756 is pictured at Doncaster shed on 10 August 1960.

Left: The final days of Barrow Hill motive power depot, prior to dieselisation, are depicted in this picture taken during the summer of 1964. Grouped around the turntable are two Ministry of Supply 'Austerity' 2-8-0s, a Kitson 0-4-0ST and an LMS Class 4 2-6-0.

Above: The interior of Doncaster Carr shed taken whilst the roof was being replaced in July 1959. Still very much an LNER atmosphere with O2s, K3s and B1s in evidence.

Below: Kings Cross top shed was renowned for lining up gleaming A3 and A4 Pacifics. However, this particular frosty morning, in the spring of 1963, found two A1s and a V2 (Nos 60144 *Kings Courier*, 60151 *Midlothian* and V2 No 60869) braving the elements and facing a very doubtful future. Sadly this famous depot closed during 1963 and steam working into Kings Cross had all but ceased by the end of 1964.

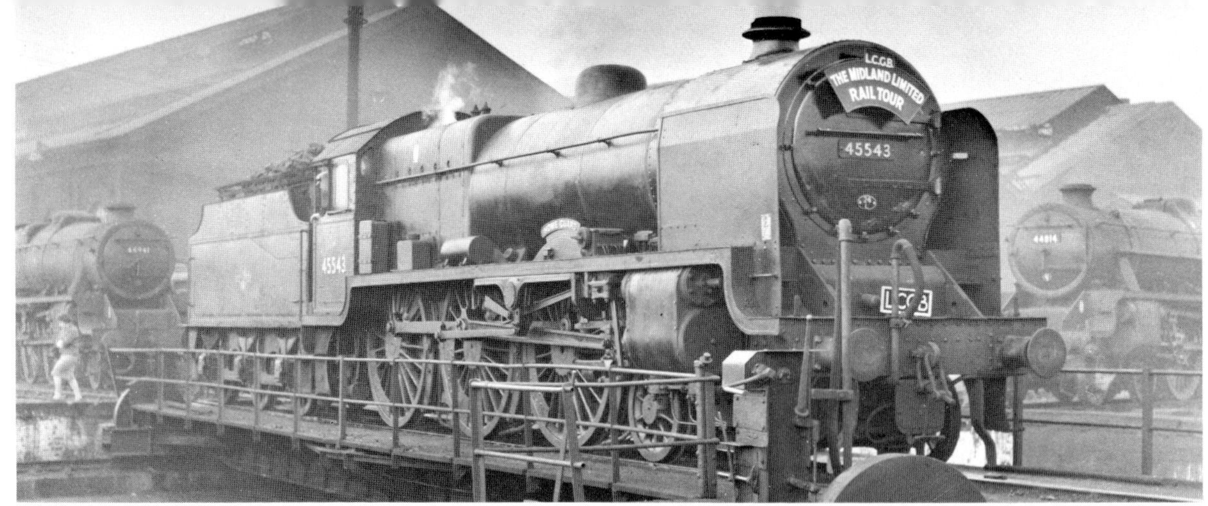

L.C.G.B.
THE MIDLAND LIMITED
RAIL TOUR
45543
45543
LCGB

30516
30516

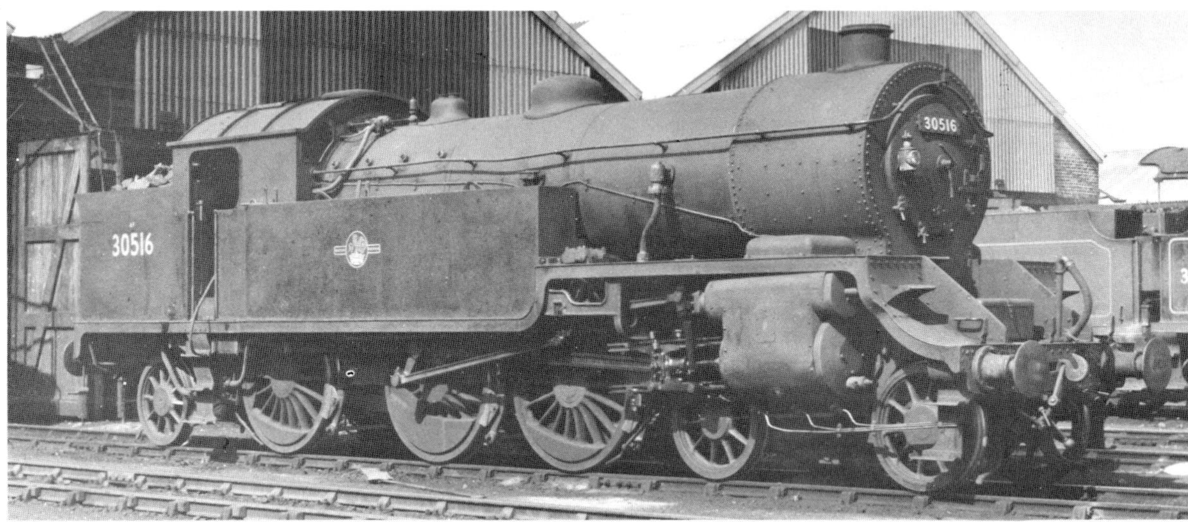

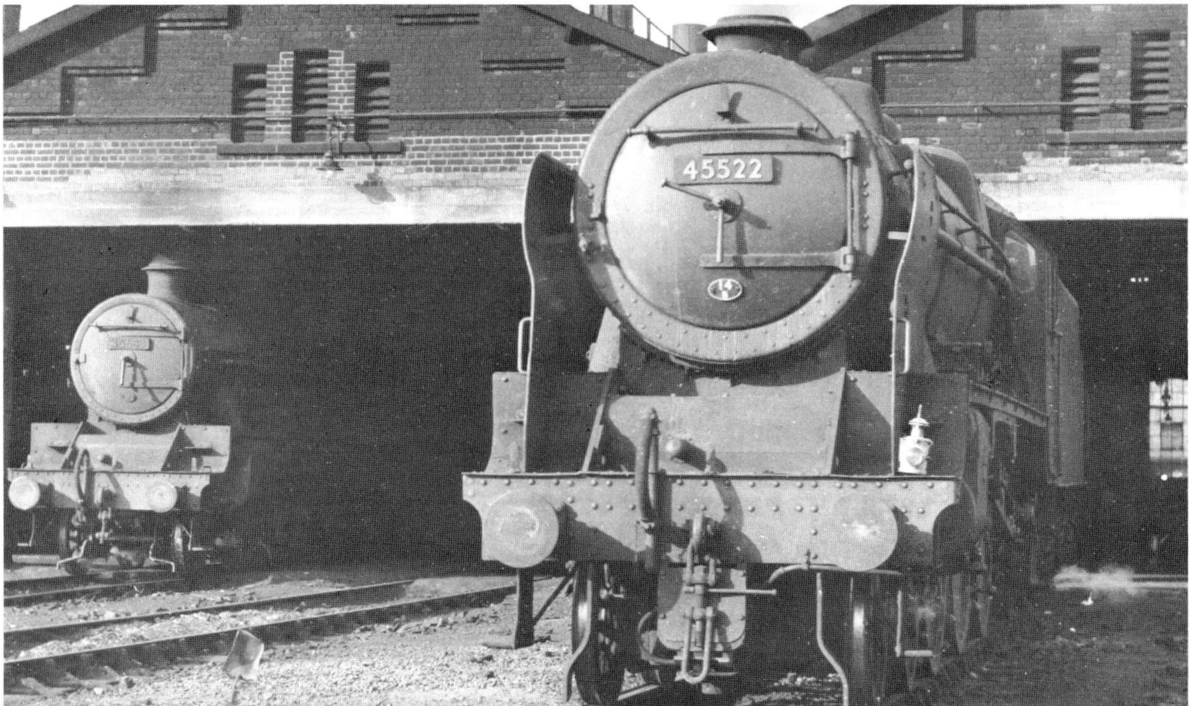
45522

Top left: The final days of the unrebuilt 'Patriots' were spent at Carnforth shed and most were withdrawn between 1960 and 1962. No 45543 *Home Guard* in unrebuilt form was one of the final pair to cease work with the introduction of the 1962 winter service. As a result she must have been taken out of store to work the LCGB tour on 7 October 1962. Photographed on the turntable at Derby shed.

Centre left: This Class H16 still bears witness to Urie's influence with its ugly stovepipe chimney. No 30516 was photographed at Eastleigh shed on 5 August 1960. They were Urie's last design before retirement, and were built in 1921/2 for the interchange traffic between Brent (Midland), Willesden (LNWR) and Feltham (LSWR).

Bottom left: On Saturday 13 August 1961 rebuilt 'Patriot' No 45522 *Prestatyn* and 'Jubilee' class No 45660 *Rooke* pulled the up 'Devonian' between Bristol and Sheffield. After this working the former was serviced at Millhouses depot where the photograph was taken. The isolation is due to the fact that the depot was about to be closed.

Above: A number of features were assessed on the 'Lord Nelson' and included: wheel diameter variations, longer boilers, extended smokeboxes, a new boiler with a combustion chamber, four beat cranks, Kylchap double blastpipes, new cylinders and Lemaitre multiple blastpipes. The latter item cured the draughting problem. No 30855 *Robert Blake* at Eastleigh shed on 5 August 1960.

Below: LMS Class 5 No 45402 and Class 2 Mogul No 46456 at Penrith depot on 9 July 1960. Penrith depot was a stabling point for engines which worked the Keswick branch and local pick-up freight trains.

Pick-Up Freights

Top: Class C 0-6-0 No 31589 pulling away from Ashford with a pick-up goods train on 20 July 1959. Introduced in 1900 these engines remained practically unaltered throughout their life. The final survivors remained at Ashford as works shunters until 1967.

Above: Class O2 2-8-0 No 63963 hurries down the GN main line with a short goods train and was photographed near Rossington on 3 May 1958. These Consolidation units were successors to Ivatt's 'Long Tom' 0-8-0s on the Peterborough coal trains.

Left: A Robinson GCR Class J11 0-6-0 No 64371, dating from 1901, saunters back to Lincoln with a rural pick-up freight train on 20 August 1958 near Washingborough. Strangely enough these fast little engines were selected by Thompson to become one of the standard designs for LNER in the 1940s.

Empty Stock Working

Top: Stanier tried his 2-6-4T with two- and three-cylinder drive but unlike Gresley found no improvement, with a result that he reverted to the former arrangement. No 42604 was a two-cylinder variant and is shown pulling the empty stock for a Euston-Manchester train past Kensal Green Cemetery on 11 March 1961.

Above: Class J50 0-6-0T No 68980 rattles out of Gasworks Tunnel with empty stock on 23 July 1959. These engines were the standard shunting tanks of the LNER, and displaced earlier Stirling and Ivatt saddle tanks which had insufficient braking power for certain duties.

Specials Abroad

Top: In 1903 the GNR seriously considered suburban electrification. As a stop-gap new engines were built, but it took three attempts to provide a suitable one in the form of the Class N2 0-6-2Ts, which survived for 40 years, and disappeared long before electrification. No 69568 is shown on a LCGB special bound for High Barnet on 2 September 1961 at Finsbury Park.

Above: On 7 October 1962 the LCGB ran a tour called the 'Midland Ltd Railtour'. The train ran from Marylebone to St Pancras via Nottingham, Burton-on-Trent and Derby. For the return trip from Derby an unrebuilt 'Patriot' No 45543 *Home Guard* was employed and is shown pulling out of Derby past Way and Works box.

Top: The outward bound 'Midland Ltd' of 7 October 1962 was propelled by a rebuilt B16 class 4-6-0 No 61438 and was photographed passing Canfield Place box having just left Finchley Road Tunnel on the climb out of Marylebone.

Above: Another interesting LCGB tour was run on 24 February 1963. It was called the 'West Countryman' and ran from Waterloo to Exeter returning via the GWR main line to Paddington. The train was hauled throughout by immaculate Class A4 No 60022 *Mallard* shown here passing through Raynes Park station.

Station Pilots

Above: Class J6 0-6-0 No 64277 drawing empty stock out of Leeds Central past B box on 8 August 1959. Originally designed for mixed traffic working, but unsuccessful in this role as relatively high speeds led to high rates of flange and axlebox wear, plus excessive hammerblow on the track. This trend led to the adoption of pony trucks for mixed traffic designs.

Below: During the late 1950s/early 1960s certain station pilots were maintained in spotless condition, or even painted in pre-Grouping livery. One such example was Class J72 0-6-0T No 68736 stationed at York. When this picture was taken on 25 June 1960, this engine had NER livery and its external condition gave no indication that she was about 60 years old.

Right: The Prairie 2-6-2T was one of several tank engine types used to draw empty stock out of Paddington and return it to the carriage sidings at Old Oak Common. Employed on such a duty is No 6125 on 27 July 1963. The majority of the 6100 class worked the suburban services out of Paddington.

Below: Class L1 2-6-4T No 67779 shunting at Kings Cross on 28 July 1959. Normally this class was employed on outer suburban work or lifting heavy empty stock trains out of Kings Cross. The design was basically a good one but their light weight and high tractive effort made them prone to slipping.

Bottom: LMS 2-6-2T No 40026 acting as the St Pancras pilot on 1 June 1962. Like a number of London suburban tanks, this engine had to be fitted with condensing apparatus to enable it to work over the Metropolitan lines to Moorgate. This class had a most undistinguished career suffering from poor front end design and insufficient boiler capacity.

Locals

Above: After nationalisation it was decided that certain LMS designs should be constructed to replace outdated motive power until the arrival of the BR standard designs. One such case was Fairburn's 2-6-4T dating from 1945, 41 of which were built at Brighton for use on the Southern Region. No 42074 pulling the 4.31pm Ashford-Maidstone East Local away from Ashford on 20 July 1959.

Below: Class D49 'Hunt' 4-4-0 No 62731 *Selkirkshire* pulling the 12.38pm York-Doncaster train past York Racecourse station on 30 August 1959. Until the arrival of the 'Schools' class in 1930 the D49 was the most powerful 4-4-0 in Britain.

Top: The use of the versatile Mogul wheel arrangement originated in North America and one of the first British versions was Churchward's design of 1911. In effect the engine was a tender version of the Class 3150 Prairie tank. No 6385 was unusual in that it was one of the batch built for the GWR by Robert Stephenson & Co. This immaculate engine is waiting to start away from Starcross with the 1.20pm Exeter St Davids-Paignton local on 11 September 1958.

Above: The Saturdays only 1.21pm Euston-Tring local passing Kensal Green Cemetery whilst in the capable hands of a Fowler 2-6-4T No 42368 on 4 March 1961.

Right: Class 1400 0-4-2T No 1421 passing Marsh Mills Junction on the 10.40am Plymouth-Tavistock south local on 7 September 1959. This engine differed only in detail from the Armstrong 517 class of 1875. Nevertheless they were capable of speeds of up to 70mph and even 80s have been claimed.

Top: Class O2 0-4-4T No 30192 shatters the tranquility of a perfect summer evening as she climbs away from Tamerton Foliot on 8 September 1959 with the 5.09pm Plymouth-Bere Alston local, having just crossed the bridge over the River Tavy, which drains into the Tamar.

Above: Another LMS design built by the Railway Executive for use on its system was the Ivatt 2-6-2T, some of which worked on the Southern Region. No 41302 lifts the lightly loaded 1pm Callington-Bere Alston local up the 1 in 42 approach to Bere Alston on 7 September 1959.

Double-Heading

Top: Fowler Class 4 2-6-4T No 42405 lends a hand to Caprotti 'Black Five' No 44738 on a special; climbing away from Leeds past Farnley Junction shed on the LNWR line to Morley and Manchester via Huddersfield on 19 July 1958.

Above: Class 2P 4-4-0 No 40585 has just joined the up 'Thames-Clyde Express' at Sheffield, to pilot a 'Black Five', No 44858, on the last leg of the run to St Pancras. The train is shown on 15 August 1959, pulling out of Sheffield Midland, and is at the foot of the 1 in 100 bank which continued for $5\frac{1}{2}$ miles.

Top: The 9.15am Plymouth-Goodrington Sands train sets off from Plymouth with 'Grange' class 4-6-0 No 6871 *Bourton Grange* piloting a 'Hall' class 4-6-0 No 6940 *Didlington Hall* on 7 September 1959.

Above: Double-heading out of Paddington was relatively rare, but on this occasion the 2.55pm to Swansea supports two 'Castles', No 5064 *Bishop's Castle* piloting No 5042 *Winchester Castle* on 4 March 1961. The location is Old Oak Common.

Top: In the mid-1950s the Midland line reintroduced the prewar mile-a-minute schedules. The 5XP timings were not very satisfactory and involved a lot of double-heading. In this instance 'Black Five' No 45426 pilots 'Jubilee' class No 45585 *Hyderabad* on the 5.10pm St Pancras-Bradford train near Elstree on 4 June 1960.

Above: Double-heading was the order of the day on the south Devon banks of the GWR main line. In this instance 'Manor' class 4-6-0 No 7808 *Cookham Manor* is piloting 'King' class 4-6-0 No 6028 *King George VI* and is approaching Hemerdon Summit with the 9.30am Paddington-Newquay on 5 September 1959

Waiting for the Road

Above: 'Castle' class No 5041 *Tiverton Castle* pauses at Oxford before departing with a Hereford-Paddington train on 9 September 1962.

Right: Midland 4F 0-6-0 No 44421 framed in a signal gantry at Spondon Junction, Derby, on 11 October 1961.

44421

Above: 'Modified Hall' class 4-6-0 No 7921 *Edstone Hall* waiting to depart from No 1 platform at Paddington with the 2.20pm Sunday parcels train to Swindon on 9 September 1962.

Right: The 2.47pm Oxford-Princes Risborough local on 8 September 1962, waiting for the road at Oxford with a GWR Prairie 2-6-2T No 6150 at the head-end.

Saddles and Panniers

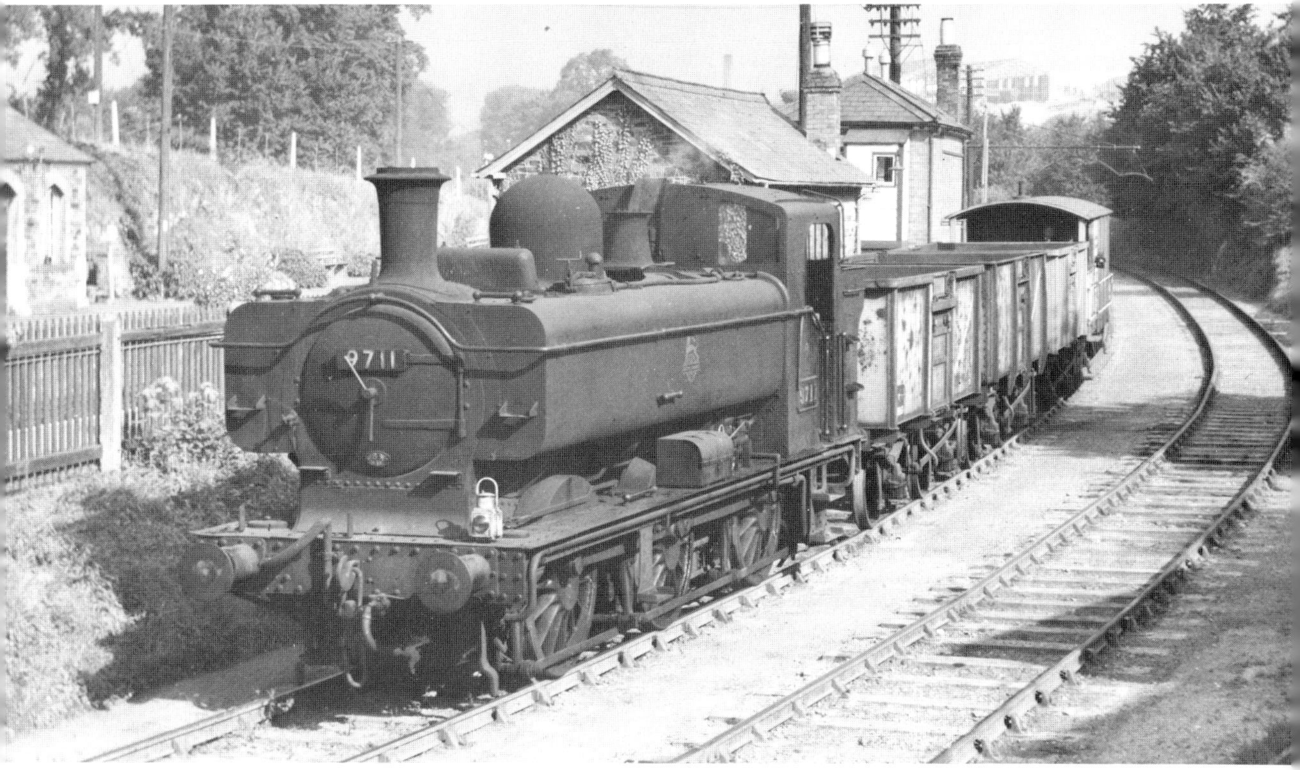

Above: No 9711 was one of the class of 863 pannier tanks developed from the 2721 class. Some of these engines were equipped with condensing gear to work over the LTE Metropolitan line. On 7 September 1959 No 9711 found herself in charge of a pick-up freight between Plymouth and Tavistock, and was photographed at Marsh Mills station.

Below: Departmental Loco No 2 Class J52 (ex-No 68816) at Doncaster Plant works on 23 May 1959. Basically tank engines had four options for storing water: a saddle tank straddling the top of the boiler, pannier tanks supported on the side of the boiler, side tanks mounted on the footplate or a well tank between the frames.

Summer Saturday at Hemerdon

Above: 'Manor' No 7820 *Dinmore Manor* piloting BR Class 9F No 92223 on the 8.05am Newquay-Newcastle on 5 September 1959. A Swindon-built double-chimneyed 9F finds itself at the head-end of a through train to the north as was often the case on summer Saturdays.

Below: 'Castle' class No 5029 *Nunney Castle* piloting BR Class 5 No 73023 on the 10.20am Penzance-Swansea train on 5 September 1959. The picture was taken at the summit of Hemerdon bank by Hemerdon Sidings box. Hemerdon bank was not the steepest bank that eastbound trains had to mount, but it was difficult in that a cold engine would start off from Plymouth faced with a 1 in 42 bank for approximately two miles in the first seven.

Above: 'County' class 4-6-0 No 1021 *County of Montgomery* pulling the 12.35pm Plymouth-Newton Abbot local on 5 September 1959. The 'Counties' were basically 'Halls' with increased boiler pressure, but the value of the latter appears to have been in doubt as they were converted back to 225lb/sq in. This engine was also the last 'County' to run with a single chimney.

Below: 'Grange' No 6870 *Bodicote Grange* piloting 4700 class 2-8-0 No 4708 on the 8.20am Penzance-Paddington train on 5 September 1959. Another freight engine which frequently appeared on summer Saturday passenger turns was Churchward's 2-8-0 of 1919. These very successful engines were his last design and were built to work the heavily loaded vacuum fitted freights.

Cross-Country Miscellany

Above: Class S15 4-6-0 No 30834 pulling out of Eastleigh with an unidentified train of Midland and Western stock on 5 August 1960. In 1920 Urie introduced a mixed traffic version of his N15 class with smaller wheels. The engine pictured here is one of a later batch, developed by Maunsell in 1927, which utilised a higher boiler pressure and a six-wheeled tender.

Below: 'Lord Nelson' class 4-6-0 No 30857 *Lord Howe* pulling the 8.37am Newcastle-Poole train away from Oxford on 8 September 1962, during her last month of active service. In 1936 this engine was built with a special boiler which included a combustion chamber. The purpose being to evaluate the boiler design for Maunsell's Pacific.

Above: N15 class 'King Arthur' No 30800 *Sir Meleaus de Lile* coasting through Eastleigh by Allbrook box on 6 August 1960. The train is the 6.05am Birmingham (Snow Hill)-Bournemouth West. The 'Arthurs' were beautiful machines as were most of Maunsell's designs and their names were romantically linked with the West Country for publicity purposes.

Below: The K3 class caused a minor stir when introduced in 1920 as a mixed traffic engine. These highly successful engines were rough to ride, but during the 1920s they were sometimes called upon to work 500-600 ton passenger trains at 70mph. This photograph shows No 61960 on the 6.46am York-Yarmouth at Washingborough near Lincoln on 22 August 1959.

Pennine Junction

Above: The picture photographers dream about; but in point of fact the likelihood of it occurring by chance were about 1 in 500. 'Royal Scot' No 46113 *Cameronian* pulling the up 'Waverley' and being overhauled by the 5.25pm Sheffield-Derby local in the capable hands of BR Class 4 4-6-0 No 75064. The picture being taken on the 1 in 100 gradient out of Sheffield Midland.

Below: BR Class 2 2-6-0 No 78023 trundles out of Sheffield past Queens Road box with an up freight on 28 May 1960. This class of engine was Ivatt's Class 2 with detail alterations. The later design popularised the tender cab with an inset coal bunker to improve vision when running bunker first.

Above: The Fowler 4F class was truly a maid-of-all-work despite its shortcomings. In fact, the operating department regarded them as ideal considering the weight and width limitations imposed on their sidings. In this instance No 44446 chugs out of Sheffield Midland with the 12.08pm Cudworth-Chesterfield local on 27 May 1961.

Below: The Class 2P 4-4-0 was an inferior machine which was the result of Derby's insistence on retaining all things Midland. The front end layout was poor and not in accordance with the accepted practice of the day. Its only claim to fame was that its maintenance costs/mile had no equal on the LMS. No 40682 ambles into Midland station with the 5.40pm local from Chesterfield on 15 August 1959.

The Serenity of Sonning

Left: 'Castle' No 5057 *Earl of Waldegrave* recovers from a signal check in Sonning Cutting whilst in charge of the 9.15am Paddington-Hereford train on 27 June 1962. Like many other designs the 'Castles' never really re-established their prewar performance; although the double chimney helped to redress the balance considerably.

Below: A 5700 class 0-6-0PT bustles through Sonning Cutting with an up goods train on 4 August 1962. No 7749 was one of 1,250 such engines introduced by Collett and Hawksworth. The pannier feature dated back to a 4-4-0T of 1898, and would have been employed by Churchward had his 0-8-0T been built.

Above: The 'Hall' class of 1924, like the 'Grange', was a direct descendant of Churchward's 'Saint' class but with a different wheel diameter. Even Hawksworth's 'Modified Hall' of 1944 only included a bar frame bogie and detail alterations. In this picture 4900 class 'Hall' No 5943 *Elmdon Hall* is shown on the 11.10am Oxford-Paddington train in Sonning Cutting on 22 July 1959.

Below: 2800 class 2-8-0 No 3806 pulling an up freight through Sonning Cutting on 22 July 1959. Two interesting features are first the segmental plate on the footplate which supported the boiler should it be necessary to remove inside cylinders and smokebox saddle; and secondly the retention of a cross-head vacuum pump which was tested by many other railways and more often than not discontinued.

Above: Like so many GWR engines, the 'Prairie' tanks continued to be produced in batches until after nationalisation. The prototype 3100 class appeared in 1903 and successors followed, incorporating detail alterations, until 1949. No 6164 was one of a batch produced in 1935 with a higher boiler pressure, and was employed on the London suburban service until the mid-1950s. It is seen here in Sonning Cutting on 2 June 1962.

Below: The beauty of Sonning which attracted so many photographers is well illustrated in this picture of 'Castle' No 7007 *Great Western* on the up 'Cathedrals Express' on the 27 June 1962.

The Mystique of Shap

Above: The 'Princess Royal' prototypes were not an immediate success due to the fact that Stanier followed his GWR experience and used a low superheat boiler. A larger superheater solved the problem, and Collett failed to heed Stanier's warning about their boiler design weakness. No 46200 *The Princess Royal* on a Carlisle-Willesden milk train at Shap Wells on 18 June 1961.

Below: Class 5F 2-6-0 No 42977 with a down freight at Shap Wells on 24 June 1961. These rather undistinguished and elusive engines were a natural successor to the Fowler Class 4F, and this must have been in Stanier's mind when he planned them as his first standard design for the LMS. In reality they were totally overshadowed by the 'Black Fives' and 'Crabs'.

Above: This 'Princess Coronation' 4-6-2, No 46234 *Duchess of Abercorn*, makes an impressive sight approaching Eamont Viaduct on the northern slope of Shap on 22 July 1961 with the 10.05am Glasgow-Birmingham train. This type of engine was a direct development of the 'Princess' class Pacific and was built to work the 300 ton high speed trains of 1937.

Below: One of Stanier's two-cylinder 2-6-4Ts No 42594 scampers down Shap near Shap village with a Tebay-Carlisle special on 8 July 1960.

Westward Ho!

Above: Rebuilt 'West Country' class 4-6-2 No 34028 *Eddystone* gathers speed after stopping at Sidmouth Junction with the 8.15am Plymouth-Waterloo train on 10 September 1958. Bulleid's Pacifics were costly to run and maintain and this led to a rebuilding programme which commenced in 1956, and produced an equally good engine.

Left: Unrebuilt 'Merchant Navy' class 4-6-2 No 35024 *East Asiatic Company* hauling the up 'Atlantic Coast Express' near Sidmouth Junction on 10 September 1958. These Pacifics were noted for their speed, acceleration and free steaming qualities with indifferent coal.

Below: Class N 2-6-0 No 31833 on the Plymouth portion of the up 'Atlantic Coast Express' near Tamerton Foliot on 10 September 1959. This engine was built at Ashford in 1924/5 from parts manufactured at Woolwich Arsenal for what was intended to be the first standard design for the proposed nationalised railway system. However, the scheme fell by the wayside and various railways, including the Southern, purchased the components and built the engines.

Lakeland Junction

Top left: The Keswick portion of the up 'Lakes Express' leaving Penrith with a Fairburn 2-6-4T in charge, namely No 42238, on 17 June 1961. Also in the picture is an Ivatt 2-6-0 No 46432 which drew the train in from Keswick.

Left: The ancestry of the 'Jubilees' was good and although their indifferent steaming was greatly improved by early superheater modifications, their performance remained rather erratic. The boiler was of GWR 'Star' and 'Saint' origin, whilst the frame was modelled on the successful 'Scot/Patriot' designs. No 45655 *Keith* gets underway with the 9.18am (SO) Keswick-Crewe-Manchester train at Penrith on 22 July 1961.

Above: Saturday morning rush-hour at Penrith on 22 July 1961. 'Black Five' No 45197 waits to depart with a Carlisle-Harrison's Sidings freight, whilst a 'Mickey Mouse' Mogul No 46455 awaits its next turn of duty. To add to the bustle Class 4F No 44126 is shunting in the sidings adjacent to the station.

Right: The introduction of the 'Royal Scot' class was interesting as Fowler had hoped to produce a compound version of Hughes' proposed Pacific. However, the operating department had decided upon a 4-6-0 and tested out a 'Castle' to prove their point and eventually won the day. In this picture No 46126 *Royal Army Service Corps* is about to leave Penrith station with the 8.20am Carlisle-Birmingham train on 24 June 1961.

Seaside Commuters

Above: 'Schools' class 4-4-0 No 30934 *St Lawrence* restarting the 4.58pm Dover Priory-London Bridge train after stopping at Ashford on 18 April 1960. The 'Schools' boiler was to have been based on that of the 'Lord Nelson' class, but the Belpaire firebox so restricted vision that it was modelled on the round top boiler of the 'King Arthur'. The result was the most powerful 4-4-0 in the world and a brilliant engine.

Below: Maunsell's Class N 2-6-0 and its 2-6-4T 'River' class twin formed the basis for his U and U1 Moguls which followed in 1928/31. These engines had larger wheels and the latter had three cylinders. They were intended as intermediate passenger engines, and were very successful in this role. A U1 class No 31894 with the 11.50am (SO) Victoria-Ramsgate train near St Mary Cray on 4 April 1959.

Left: The L1 class 4-4-0s were designed to handle the 80min expresses to Folkestone, and unlike the E1 and D1 class 4-4-0s they were a SECR design which did not benefit from Maunsell's attention to valve gear. The latter were excellent engines and worked the continental expresses till the mid-1920s. No 31788 on an up Kent coast excursion on 4 August 1958 photographed between Faversham and Teynham.

Below: A 'German' at speed. In 1914 the SECR had to resort to ordering 20 4-4-0s from the Borsig Company in Germany. Hence, the nickname. Class L No 31780 with an up Kent Coast express on 23 August 1958 near Sittingbourne.

Bottom: With electrification only three months away 'Battle of Britain' class No 34085 *501 Squadron* puts in a brave appearance on a relief to the 9.35am Victoria-Ramsgate train. Photographed near Faversham on 28 March 1959. The preoccupation with war had led the Southern to adopt names of battles for their new Pacific. Eventually this idea was dropped; however, on the lightweight versions they named some after Battle of Britain squadrons.

West Riding Interchange

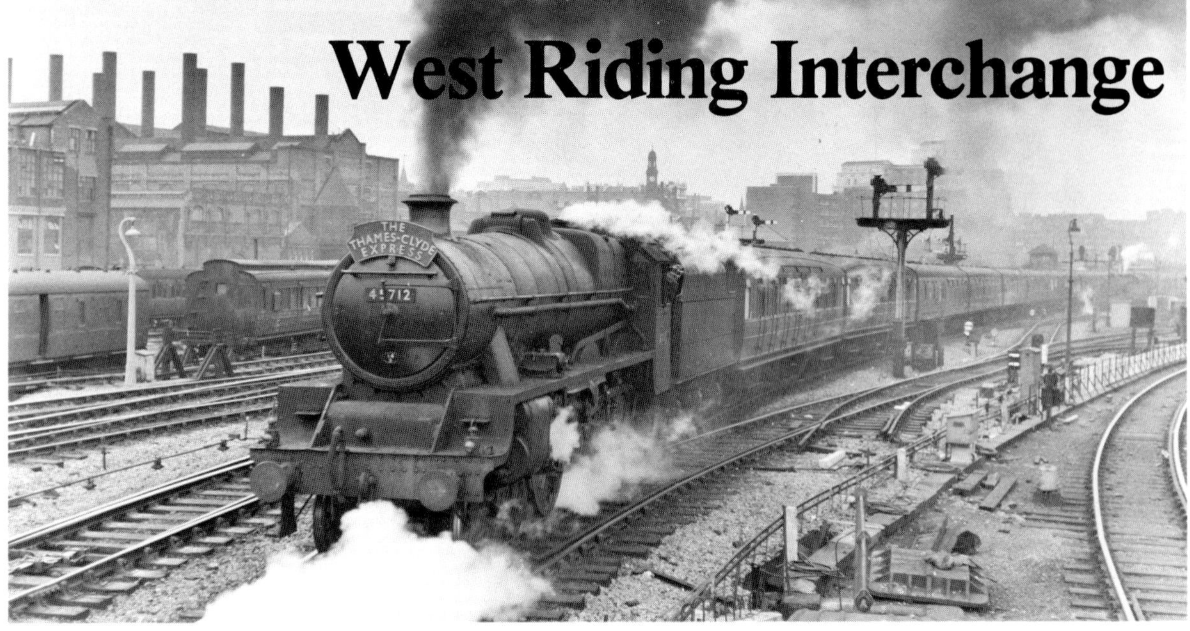

Above: The up 'Thames-Clyde Express' leaving Leeds City station behind one of Kentish Town's 'Jubilees' No 45712 *Victory* on 13 August 1960. The fact that the cylinder cocks are open suggests that the boiler was priming, which was a problem with some of these engines.

Left: The reason for the 'Crabs' ungainly appearance stems from the fact that Hughes did not approve of high boiler pressure ie above 180lb/sq in; with a result that he had to use large diameter cylinders, to obtain the necessary power, which then had to be lifted to clear the loading gauge. No 42713 is pulling a South Shields-Manchester train on 4 July 1959.

Top right: 8F class 2-8-0 No 48158 heading north past Wortley Junction signalbox with a freight on 16 August 1959. This engine was one of a batch built at Crewe in 1943 and might have served overseas during World War II; many did and some remained in Turkey, Iraq and Egypt.

Centre right: An immaculate 'Green Arrow', Class V2 No 60901, leaving Leeds with the 5.38pm Manchester-Newcastle train. Photographed at Wortley Junction on 4 July 1959. Built for the 'Green Arrow' freight service in 1936, these successful engines were the first 2-6-2 tender engines to run in this country, and caused Gresley to abandon any ideas of a new 4-6-0 design for the LNER.

Bottom right: B1 class No 61214 pulling the 6.16pm Leeds Central-Kings Cross train past B box on 19 June 1961. The efficient steaming of the parallel boilered B1s and 'Schools' threw doubt into the Swindon argument that a taper boiler with the Belpaire firebox was the best choice. The latter was more expensive to produce and cheaper to maintain, but the locomotive exchanges proved that the B1 parallel boiler was as efficient as the taper variety on the 'Black Five'.

60901
60901

WHITEHALL

Notorious Inclines

Left: Unfitted freights had to halt at the top of the Lickey Incline so that a proportion of the wagon brakes could be pinned down. In this photograph a 'Crab' No 42764 has just halted at the summit for this purpose, whilst an unseen Class 9F ascending the 2 mile 1 in $37\frac{1}{2}$ bank is being banked by three GWR pannier tanks and a 'Jinty' on 25 July 1961.

Below: A regular summer Saturday working for a Kings Cross B1 was the Skegness run; and in this case No 61073 is seen climbing up the 1 in 107 past Holloway South Up box with the 8.10am Kings Cross-Butlins Holiday Camp special on 1 July 1961.

Top right: Class A1 No 60144 *King's Courier* belonging to Doncaster Carr shed does battle with the 10.20am Kings Cross-Hull and Leeds express on 10 June 1961 at Holloway. The A1 represented the final phase of Doncaster's Pacific development era. They achieved a level of economy and reliability hitherto unknown, but never equalled the A4s performance.

Centre right: For westbound expresses it was Dainton's 1 in 36 and Rattery bank which presented the problem; whilst eastbound trains had to contend with Hemerdon's 1 in 42. No 4976 *Warfield Hall* pilots 'King' No 6002 *King William IV* near the summit of Hemerdon on 5 September 1959 on the 9.20am St Ives-Paddington train.

Bottom right: Surprisingly enough 'Black Five' No 44673 is descending the northern side of Shap with the 8.50am Blackpool-Glasgow train on the 9 July 1960. This was a relatively modern engine having been built as late as 1950.

ADVANCE WORKS

4976

Steam Citadels

Left: The exit roads from Kings Cross were difficult to say the least; first diving below the Regents Canal in Gasworks Tunnel, with its attendant wet rail, followed by a steady climb to Finsbury Park. In this picture No 60103 *Flying Scotsman* picks her way carefully across the points, heading for Gasworks Tunnel, with the 6.05pm Kings Cross-Leeds train on 17 July 1959.

Below: Paddington station was completed in 1854 and was another of Brunel's masterpieces. The design was greatly influenced by Crystal Palace. Standing in platform 10 is 'Castle' No 5076 *Gladiator* having just drawn a Newbury race special into the terminus on 27 July 1963.

Bottom: St Pancras was a railway extravaganza epitomising the wealth of the Midland Railway and features architecture in the Gothic revival style which was popular in the 1860s. Completed in 1868 the great train hall, as it was known, had a roof span of 240ft and presents a magnificent spectacle under which No 45561 *Saskatchewan* is waiting to depart with the 4.10pm to Sheffield on 11 March 1961.

Meccas of Steam

Above: The 'Britannia' class Pacifics were designed and built at Crewe in the early 1950s and were not without introductory problems such as, cylinder damage due to priming, broken coupling rods, wheels moving on hollow axles and tenders breaking free. *Anzac* takes the Chaddesden Loop out of Derby with the 12.10pm Manchester Piccadilly-St Pancras train on 24 January 1962.

Below: Over the years Derby has increased in importance as a railway engineering centre, whilst others such as Swindon have declined or disappeared. This picture was taken from Way and Works box, to the south of Derby station, and provides a good view of the junction and the locomotive works. In the foreground Fairburn 2-6-4T No 42161 wheels the 5.50pm Derby-Nottingham local down the main line on 30 September 1961.

Above: The daily procession of steam engines being transferred between the running sheds and Doncaster Plant Works was nicknamed 'the plant stream'; and on 1 September 1961 it included two Class 4 2-6-0s Nos 43037/64, and a 'Britannia' No 70005 *John Milton*. In charge of the cavalcade is 'Austerity' 2-8-0 No 90001. Photographed from Bridge Junction box.

Below: Doncaster was very much a railway town, whilst the works was famous for its Pacific designs. One of Gresley's most striking early engines was his K3 class Mogul which paved the way for the Pacifics. No 61890 was one such engine, and is shown accelerating the 4.35pm Doncaster-Lincoln train away from Doncaster past Bridge Junction box on 1 September 1961.

Steam Amid the Gloom

Left: Lurking in one of Paddington's rare gloomy spots is 'Castle' No 5018 *St Mawes Castle* having just coupled up to the 2.20pm Paddington-Oxford train in platform No 2 on 9 September 1962.

Below left: The dark cavernous interior of St Pancras makes a backdrop for BR Class 5 No 73135 as she storms out with the 4.54pm excursion to Nottingham on Whit Monday 1958. This engine was one of the later batches which were improved by the use of Caprotti valve gear. This statement should be qualified as the 'Black Fives' so treated, were regarded as fast engines with slow acceleration rates.

Below: The 'Elizabethan' bursts out of the gloom and smokey atmosphere of Kings Cross on 23 July 1959. One of top shed's immaculate A4s, No 60028 *Walter K. Whigham*, having been rostered for this duty. In 1951 the Eastern Region introduced a new non-stop express between London and Edinburgh known as the 'Capitals Limited' which was renamed the 'Elizabethan' in 1953.

Lengthening Shadows

Left: Steam shrouds hang around A4 No 60021 *Wild Swan* as the steam era at Kings Cross draws to a close. Steam working officially ended at the end of June; one of the last steam turns being the 4.05pm Kings Cross-Leeds train photographed here in April 1963.

Below: The busy Exmouth branch had a half hourly service to Exeter at peak periods which was worked, for many years by Drummond's M7s dating from 1897. After 1953 the load was shared by Class 2 2-6-2Ts of LMS and BR origin. These engines were regularly called upon to work seven coach trains whilst those to Sidmouth had through carriages to Waterloo. In this picture Class M7 No 30676 sets off from Exmouth with the 6.46pm to Tipton St Johns on 7 September 1958.

Bottom: Sunday 9 September 1962 saw the official termination of steam working on the Paddington-Birmingham line. Amid the lengthening shadows of the day in question a 'King' class 4-6-0 No 6022 *King Edward III* sets off from Paddington with the 5.10pm to Birmingham.

Above: A 'Princess Coronation' sparkles amid the gloom as she emerges from the dark depths of Kensal Green Tunnel, having been checked by signals whilst working the down 'Royal Scot' on 18 March 1961. The engine was No 46247 *City of Liverpool.*

Below: The sun sinks on Thursday 8 June 1961 leaving two locomotives to reflect on their past glories and to face the uncertain future. The down fitted freight is in the hands of Class A4 No 60025 *Falcon*, whilst the up freight gathers speed behind K3 2-6-0 No 61965. Both are about to pass Bridge Junction box, Doncaster.